SPELLING WORKS

CREATIVE ACTIVITIES TO USE WITH ANY SPELLING LIST

GRADES 4-8

WRITTEN BY LINDA SCHWARTZ
ILLUSTRATED BY BEV ARMSTRONG

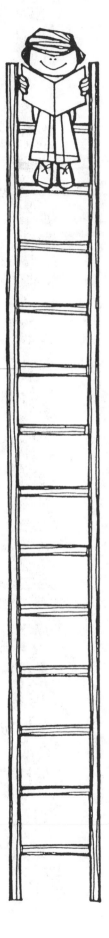

The
Learning
Works

Copyright ©1993
The Learning Works, Inc.
Santa Barbara, California 93160
Printed in the United States of America

Contents

Introduction

Spelling Works is filled with creative, challenging puzzles and activities that can be used with *any* spelling list. The flexibility of the activities makes **Spelling Works** ideal for use with your entire class, for small group instruction at a spelling center, or for individual and homework assignments. Students can select their own activities or you can assign pages to meet individual needs. (Some of the activities may be more suitable than others for dealing with specific spelling lists, but a wide range of exciting activities are here for you to choose from.)

These open-ended activities are designed to make spelling fun – from designing a spelling spacecraft to creating a spelling cheer. **Spelling Works** provides your students opportunities to explore a thesaurus and dictionary, create riddles and rebuses, decipher codes, rhyme words, design puzzles, write original stories, and lots more!

Spelling List

Write each of your spelling words below using your best handwriting.

_____   _____

_____   _____

_____   _____

_____   _____

_____   _____

_____   _____

_____   _____

_____   _____

_____   _____

_____   _____

Acrostic Verse

Pick a spelling word from your list. Use the letters in your word and write a poem describing yourself. Your poem does not have to rhyme.

Example: (spelling word – **children**)

C athy is my friend.

H er hobbies include gymnastics and collecting baseball cards.

I nterested in becoming an Olympic star.

L oves to read books, especially those

D escribing the lives of famous people.

R ed is her favorite color.

E njoys going on long bike rides on weekends.

N uts about anything chocolate.

Variations:

Using other words from your spelling list, write acrostic poems on any of these topics:

- **an animal**
- **a holiday or festival**
- **a famous person**
- **your favorite color**

Where do penguins live? In Antarctica, South America, South Africa, Australia and New Zealand.

In a penguin colony there may be a million birds.

No penguins live at the North Pole.

Though penguins can't fly, they can swim fast.

Emperor penguins carry their eggs on their feet.

Rockhopper and macaroni penguins may live together.

Alphabet Animal Stories

Pick five words from your spelling list. Cut out letters of different sizes, shapes, and colors from old magazines to spell your five words. Then arrange the cut-out letters of all five words in the shape of a make-believe animal. Glue the letters on a piece of white art paper as shown. Give the creature a clever name and write a short story about a day in the life of your animal. Write the five spelling words you used.

Example:

Five spelling words used:

1. **conclude**

2. **excavate**

3. **fragile**

4. **horizontal**

5. **territory**

Spelling Works
©1993 – The Learning Works, Inc.

Antonym Antics

Antonyms are words that have opposite meanings.
Example: generous - stingy

Select ten words from your spelling list and write them in column A. Then use your dictionary to find an antonym for each word. Write the antonym in column B. Be sure to mix the antonyms up so they are not in the same order as your spelling words. Make an answer key for your words. Then give your paper to a friend and have him or her match the spelling words with the proper antonyms. Check your friend's answers with the answer key.

COLUMN A

1._____

2._____

3._____

4._____

5._____

6._____

7._____

8._____

9._____

10. _____

COLUMN B

A._____

B. _____

C. _____

D. _____

E. _____

F._____

G. _____

H. _____

I. _____

J._____

Name _____

Bonanza Words

Using the code below, add the point value for each of your spelling words. How many Bonanza Words can you find? A **Bonanza Word** is a word that totals exactly one hundred points. Circle all of your spelling words that total one hundred points! See how many other Bonanza Words you can find in books you read or in the dictionary. Write any Bonanza Words in the bursts below.

A=1	G= 7	M=13	S=19	Y=25
B=2	H= 8	N=14	T=20	Z=26
C=3	I= 9	O=15	U=21	
D=4	J=10	P=16	V=22	
E=5	K=11	Q=17	W=23	
F=6	L=12	R=18	X=24	

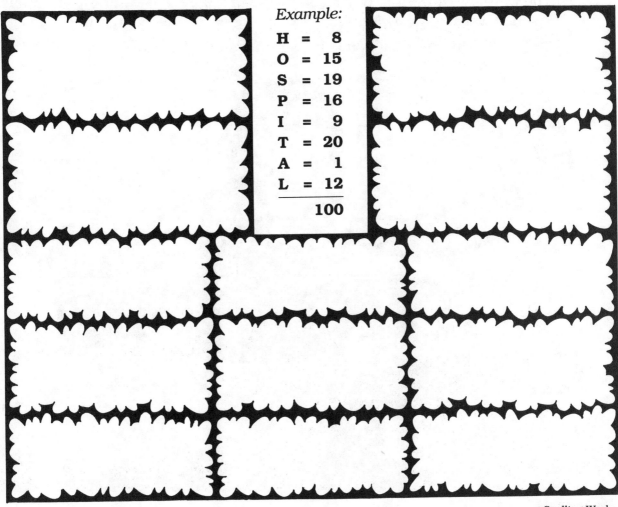

Example:

H	=	8
O	=	15
S	=	19
P	=	16
I	=	9
T	=	20
A	=	1
L	=	12
		100

Spelling Works
©1993 – The Learning Works, Inc.

Charades

To the Teacher:

Play a game of Charades using the words on the class spelling list.

Directions:

1. Duplicate as many Charade cards as you need (page 11). Write a spelling word on each card and place the cards in a basket.

2. Divide your class into two teams.

3. Decide in advance how much time the team has to guess the spelling word that is being acted out.

4. A player from one team picks a Charade card from the basket and pantomimes the spelling word for her/his team.

5. If the team guesses the word in the allotted time, they receive a point.

6. Then a player from the other team picks a Charade card and pantomimes the spelling word for her/his team. Play continues in this manner until time is up.

7. The team with the most points wins at the end of the game.

Charades
(continued)

Duplicate the Charade cards below. Write a spelling word on each card. Cut out the cards, and use them with the game described on page 10.

Spelling Works
©1993 – The Learning Works, Inc.

Create a Postcard

Think of your favorite vacation spot. Pretend you are there, and write a message to a friend on the postcard below. Use as many spelling words as you can in your message. Underline the spelling words as you go.

When you have written your message and addressed your postcard, design a postage stamp. Draw your stamp in the square on the postcard.

Create a Postcard
(continued)

Draw and color a picture of the vacation spot you described on page 12.

Spelling Works
©1993 – The Learning Works, Inc.

Create a Thesaurus

A **thesaurus** is a book that lists synonyms for words. Have fun making your own thesaurus. Write your spelling words in alphabetical order on notebook paper as shown. Then write a list of synonyms in the space below each word. Use your dictionary or an actual thesaurus for help. Design a cover for your thesaurus and give it a title.

automobile	luminous
auto	bright
car	glowing
vehicle	radiant
	shining
counterfeit	overcome
fake	conquer
false	defeat
phony	subdue
government	quiver
control	shake
regulation	shiver
rule	tremble
	vibrate
journey	squelch
expedition	crush
trip	silence
voyage	stifle

Detect an Accent

When a word has more than one syllable, one of the syllables is said with more force than the others. An **accent mark** (′) is placed after that syllable.

Example: prin′ - ci - pal

Using your spelling list, find words that fit the following categories. Write the words on the lines provided. Use your dictionary if you need help.

Words with the accent
on the **first** syllable

_____

_____

_____

_____

Words with the accent
on the **second** syllable

_____

_____

_____

_____

Words with the accent
on the **third** syllable

_____

_____

_____

_____

Words with the accent
on the **fourth** syllable

_____

_____

_____

_____

oys-ter catch-er

Spelling Works
©1993 – The Learning Works, Inc.

Illustrate a Word

Pretend a company that publishes a popular student dictionary asks you to illustrate the words on your spelling list for their next edition. Write a spelling word under each box. Illustrate the words in the spaces provided. Use the back of your paper if you need more room.

Example:

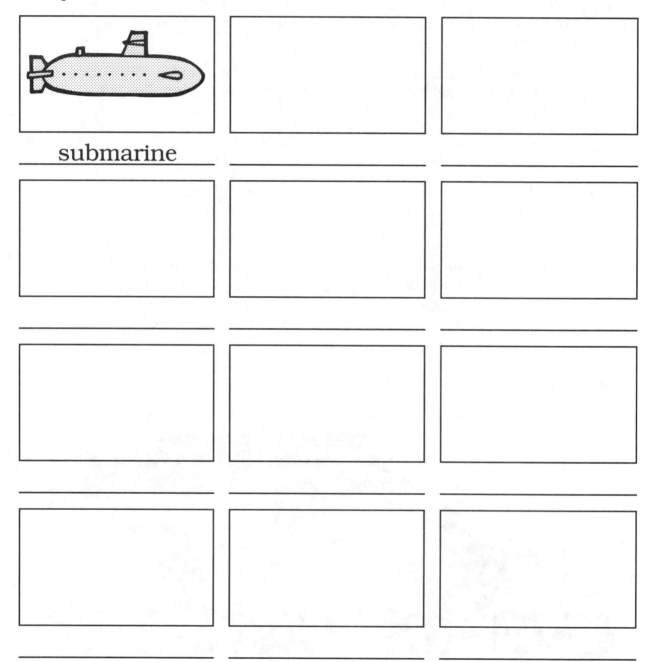

submarine _____

Futuristic Car

Design and color a car of the future on white art paper. Use as many spelling words as you can to write a magazine advertisement for your car. Underline your spelling words as you use them.

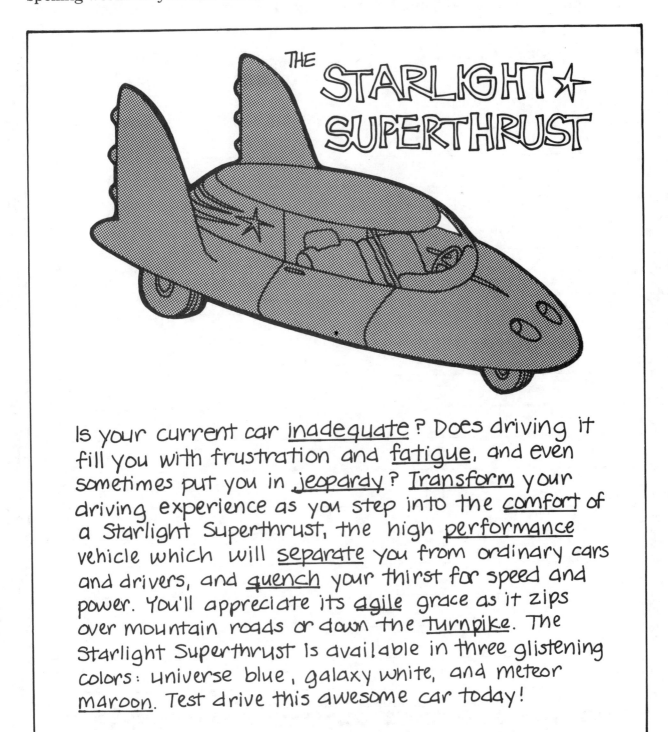

THE **STARLIGHT☆ SUPERTHRUST**

Is your current car <u>inadequate</u>? Does driving it fill you with frustration and <u>fatigue</u>, and even sometimes put you in <u>jeopardy</u>? <u>Transform</u> your driving experience as you step into the <u>comfort</u> of a Starlight Superthrust, the high <u>performance</u> vehicle which will <u>separate</u> you from ordinary cars and drivers, and <u>quench</u> your thirst for speed and power. You'll appreciate its <u>agile</u> grace as it zips over mountain roads or down the <u>turnpike</u>. The Starlight Superthrust is available in three glistening colors: universe blue, galaxy white, and meteor <u>maroon</u>. Test drive this awesome car today!

Spelling Works
©1993 – The Learning Works, Inc.

Newspaper Hunt

Write your spelling words on the lines below. Search through newspapers to see how many of your spelling words you can find. Each time you find one of the words on your spelling list, cut it out and tape it next to your word. (Be sure everyone in your family has finished reading the newspaper before you begin cutting.)

Spelling Words	Newspaper Words
_____	_____
_____	_____
_____	_____
_____	_____
_____	_____
_____	_____
_____	_____
_____	_____
_____	_____
_____	_____
_____	_____
_____	_____
_____	_____
_____	_____
_____	_____
_____	_____
_____	_____

Note This

Write a phone message to a friend. Use at least ten of the words on your spelling list. Underline each word as you use it in your message.

To _____

From _____

Date _____ **Time** _____

Phone Number _____

Message _____

_____

_____

_____

_____

_____

_____

_____

_____

_____

Spelling Works
©1993 – The Learning Works, Inc.

Parts of Speech Pizzas

Find examples of nouns, verbs, adjectives, and adverbs from the words on your spelling list. Write examples of each in the pizzas below.

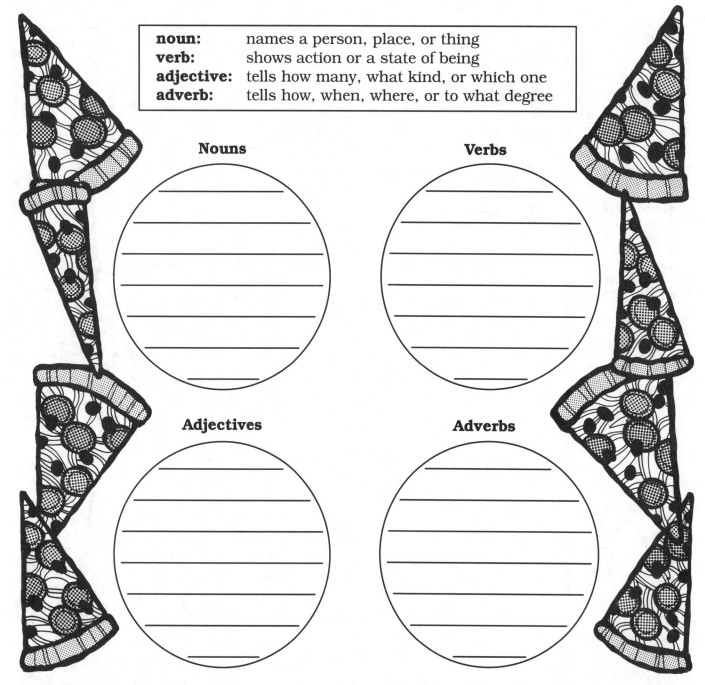

noun:	names a person, place, or thing
verb:	shows action or a state of being
adjective:	tells how many, what kind, or which one
adverb:	tells how, when, where, or to what degree

Nouns

Verbs

Adjectives

Adverbs

On a separate piece of paper, write a humorous story about a new pizza restaurant with a very unusual kind of pizza on the menu. Use as many of your spelling words as you can. Underline the spelling words in your story.

Pick a Pair

Directions:

1. Write each of your spelling words <u>twice</u> on blank, 3" x 5" index cards, one word per card.

2. Shuffle all the cards and place them face down in even rows on a large table or on the floor.

3. To play "Pick a Pair" with a classmate, take turns picking two cards looking for a pair of words. When you find two cards with the same spelling word, keep the pair and take another turn.

4. If you pick two cards that do <u>not</u> have the same word, replace them face down where you found them. It is then your friend's turn to pick.

5. Play continues in this manner until all of the cards have been taken. The person with the most pairs is the winner.

Spelling Works
©1993 – The Learning Works, Inc.

Pickle

Write a story using as many words as you can from your spelling list. When you come to a spelling word, substitute the word **pickle** instead. Underline the word **pickle** each time you use it. On a separate piece of paper, alphabetize all of the words on your spelling list. When you have finished, exchange stories and spelling lists with a classmate. See if your classmate can pick the correct spelling word each time the word **pickle** appears in your story. Ask your friend to write the missing spelling word above the word **pickle.**

_____
(title)

_____

_____

_____

_____

_____

_____

_____

_____

_____

Prefix Pet

A **prefix** is a syllable added to the beginning of a word. A prefix changes the meaning of a word.

Examples:

anti-	against, opposite of	antifreeze, antisocial
bi-	two	bicycle, bifocals
dis-	not, opposite of, reverse	distrust, disorder
pre-	before or at an earlier time, in front of	premature, preview
quadr-	four	quadrangle, quadruplet
re-	again, back	review, return
tri-	three	triangle, tricycle, trimester
un-	not, lack of, reverse	unhappy, unrest, undo
uni-	one	unicycle, unicorn

Look over your spelling words and list all the prefixes you find. Draw a Prefix Pet on a separate piece of white art paper. Give your pet a name. Use the prefixes from your spelling list to write a description of your pet.

Prefix   Spelling Word

_____   _____

_____   _____

_____   _____

_____   _____

_____   _____

_____   _____

Example:

This is an unhappy, disorganized, uni-winged, bi-headed, quadruped.

Spelling Works
©1993 – The Learning Works, Inc.

Puzzle Search

Make a Puzzle Search for a friend.

1. Write as many of your spelling words as you can in the grid on the opposite page. Your words can be written vertically, horizontally, or diagonally.

2. List each spelling word that you use on the lines provided on page 25.

3. Write letters in the empty boxes in the grid.

4. Give the puzzle and a copy of the spelling list to a friend. Have your friend circle all the spelling words in the puzzle and on the list as he/she finds them.

Puzzle Search

(continued)

SPELLING LIST

_____   _____

_____   _____

_____   _____

_____   _____

_____   _____

_____   _____

Spelling Works
©1993 – The Learning Works, Inc.

Rhyme Creature

Write your spelling words below. Use the back of the paper if more space is needed. Next to each word, write words that rhyme.

Example: **CREATURE:** teacher, preacher, feature

spelling word	rhyming word/words
1. _____	_____
2. _____	_____
3. _____	_____
4. _____	_____
5. _____	_____
6. _____	_____
7. _____	_____
8. _____	_____
9. _____	_____
10. _____	_____
11. _____	_____
12. _____	_____

Riddle Riot

Write riddles or jokes below using words on your spelling list. Share your creations with your classmates.

Example: (for the spelling word - **polygon**)

    Q. What do you call a parrot that is lost?
    A. A polygon

Roundup

Write your spelling words in alphabetical order. (Use the back of your paper if necessary.) Number your words. Circle the words following the numbers that are divisible by 3. Write these words in the lasso.

Scrambled Spelling

Write your spelling words in the box below. Then choose ten words and scramble the letters. Write the scrambled words in the eggs, one word per egg. Do not write the scrambled words in the same order they appear in the box. Give your scrambled words to a friend to unscramble and write correctly on a separate piece of paper.

Example: sentence = teenscen

Shaperoos

Select one of the shapes below or create your own design. Draw it as large as you can on a piece of white art paper. Write your spelling words within the shape. Draw dots between the words to separate them.

Example:

Spacecraft Spelling

Design and color a spacecraft on a piece of white art paper. Then write a short story about your vehicle using as many of your spelling words as you can. Underline the spelling words as you use them in your story. Glue your story underneath your design as shown below.

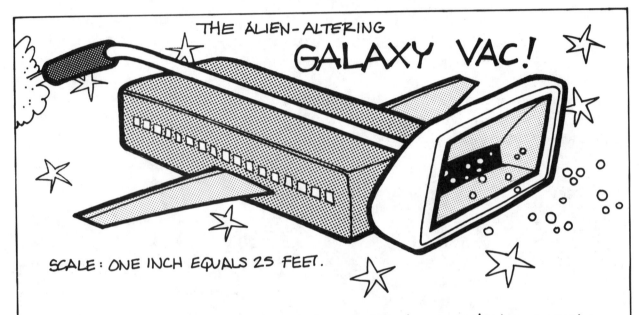

THE ALIEN-ALTERING
GALAXY VAC!

SCALE: ONE INCH EQUALS 25 FEET.

This <u>unique</u> spacecraft is designed to <u>regulate</u> <u>unruly</u> aliens while helping its owner get rich. It will <u>function</u> as a powerful vacuum cleaner, sucking its <u>quarry</u> in through the <u>massive</u> front opening. Passing through tubes in the spacecraft's <u>laboratory</u>, <u>individual</u> aliens will be miniaturized until they are only a few inches tall. Then, with a <u>surge</u> of power, they will be plasticized, every hideous detail of their bodies preserved for <u>eternity</u>. Huge bins in the spacecraft will hold millions of these now-harmless creatures. Later, on Earth, cereal manufacturers will <u>eagerly</u> purchase these weird, multicolored aliens for <u>distribution</u> to people who enjoy finding ugly plastic things floating around in their breakfast.

Spelling Works
©1993 – The Learning Works, Inc.

Name _____

Spelling Cheer

On a separate piece of paper, write cheers for ten of your spelling words.

Example: spelling word - **celebrate**

> **Celebrate, celebrate,**
> **Spell it right and you'll feel great.**
> **C-E-L-E-brate, brate, brate**
> **It's easy to spell celebrate!**

Teach your cheers to a group of friends in your class. Practice performing your favorites, and then present them to the whole class as a fun way of reviewing your spelling words prior to a test.

Super Scavenger Hunt

Can you find words from your spelling list that fit each of these descriptions?

1. a word that starts and ends with a vowel _____

2. a word that starts and ends with the same letter _____

3. a word that starts and ends with a consonant _____

4. a plural word _____

5. a word that begins with a prefix _____

6. a word that ends with a suffix _____

7. a compound word _____

8. an eight-letter word _____

9. a word that has more than one meaning _____

10. a word with smaller words of three or more letters inside such as **combination.**
    (comb, bin, nation)

_____

11. a word with two of the same vowels together such as **eerie** _____

12. a word with two of the same consonants together such as **o<u>tt</u>er** _____

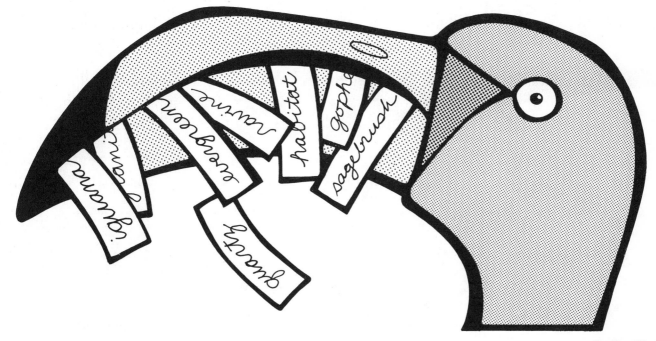

Syllable Count

Each word defined in a dictionary is called an entry word. It is printed in bold, dark letters. Entry words are divided into syllables. Your dictionary may use a dot, a dash, or a space to divide a word into syllables.

Syllables help you say words correctly. They also help you break a long word when you cannot fit the whole word on one line while writing.

Divide the words on your spelling list into syllables. Use your dictionary if you need help. Write the words under the proper headings.

Words with one syllable

_____
_____
_____
_____
_____
_____

Words with two syllables

_____
_____
_____
_____
_____
_____

Words with three syllables

_____
_____
_____
_____
_____
_____

Words with four or more syllables

_____
_____
_____
_____
_____
_____
_____

os • ten • ta • tious • ness

Symbol Spelling

A **symbolic code** is one in which a random symbol is used to stand for a letter of the alphabet.

Example:

A	B	C	D	E	F	G	H	I	J	K	L	M

N	O	P	Q	R	S	T	U	V	W	X	Y	Z

Select ten words from your spelling list. Write these words on a separate piece of paper using the symbolic code above. Give your paper to a friend. See if your friend can identify and spell the words correctly. Try making up your own symbolic code and writing a message using the words from your spelling list.

Spelling Works
©1993 – The Learning Works, Inc.

Synonym Sandwiches

Synonyms are words that are spelled and pronounced differently but have similar meanings. Select twelve spelling words and write them in the top half of each sandwich, one word per sandwich. Use a dictionary or a thesaurus and list a synonym for each word in the bottom half of the sandwich.

Example:

identical (your spelling word)

same (synonym)

Tic-Tac-Toe Spelling Code

The Tic-Tac-Toe Code is based on the positions of letters within a tic-tac-toe grid and within the spaces formed by an X. Each letter is represented by the lines that define the space the letter occupies.

Example: ∨̇ ⌐| ⊡ ∧ = **warm**

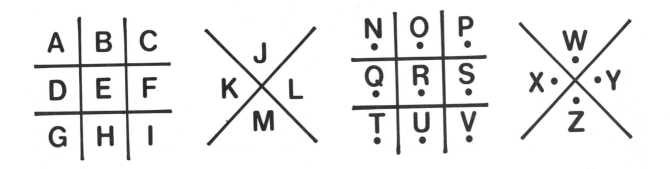

Use the words on your spelling list to make up a Tic-Tac-Toe Code message for a classmate to solve on a separate piece of paper. Use the symbols above instead of the letters. (See the example.) Once you get the idea, try writing entire sentences in Tic-Tac-Toe Code using words from your spelling list.

Try a Trio

Write your spelling words and number them on a separate piece of paper. Then choose three words from your list that are next to numbers that appear in your telephone number. Use these spelling words in a story or poem. Underline the three words as you use them in your writing.

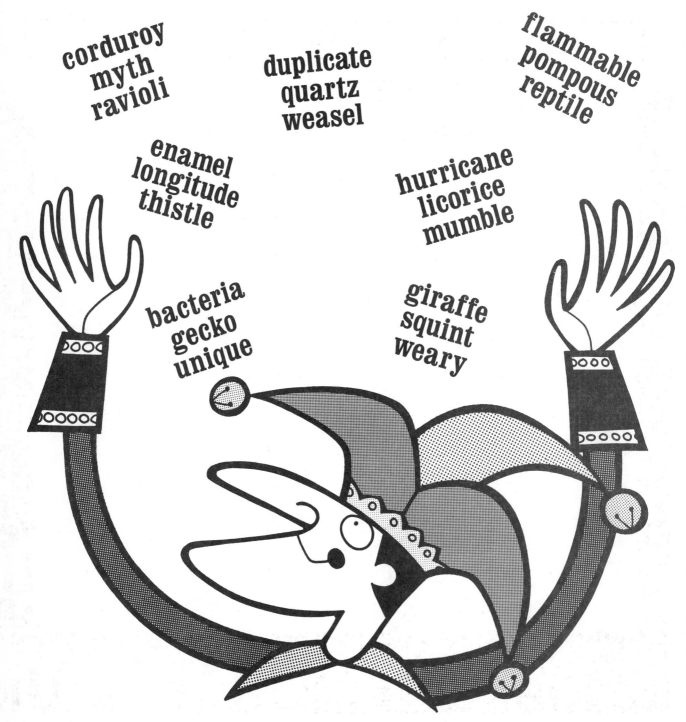

corduroy
myth
ravioli

duplicate
quartz
weasel

flammable
pompous
reptile

enamel
longitude
thistle

hurricane
licorice
mumble

bacteria
gecko
unique

giraffe
squint
weary

Vowel Code

Write twelve spelling words in column A. Then substitute the number code below for each vowel and write the coded word in column B. Do not write the coded words in the same order as they appear in column A. Give your list to a friend. Have her/him match the codes to the correct spelling words as shown.

A = 5	E = 4	I = 3	O = 2	U = 1

Example: __Z__ delicious   Z. D4L3C321S

COLUMN A	COLUMN B
____ 1._____	A. _____
____ 2._____	B. _____
____ 3._____	C. _____
____ 4._____	D. _____
____ 5._____	E. _____
____ 6._____	F. _____
____ 7._____	G. _____
____ 8._____	H. _____
____ 9._____	I. _____
____ 10._____	J. _____
____ 11._____	K. _____
____ 12._____	L. _____

Wacky Sentences

Use each of your spelling words in a sentence. Try to use words that start with the same letter as your spelling word. Be sure to underline your spelling word in each sentence. Use the back of your paper if necessary. Illustrate your two favorite sentences in the boxes below.

Example: spelling word - **frightened**

Five frivolous ferrets <u>frightened</u> four floundering fleas.

_____

_____

_____

_____

_____

_____

_____

_____

_____

_____

_____

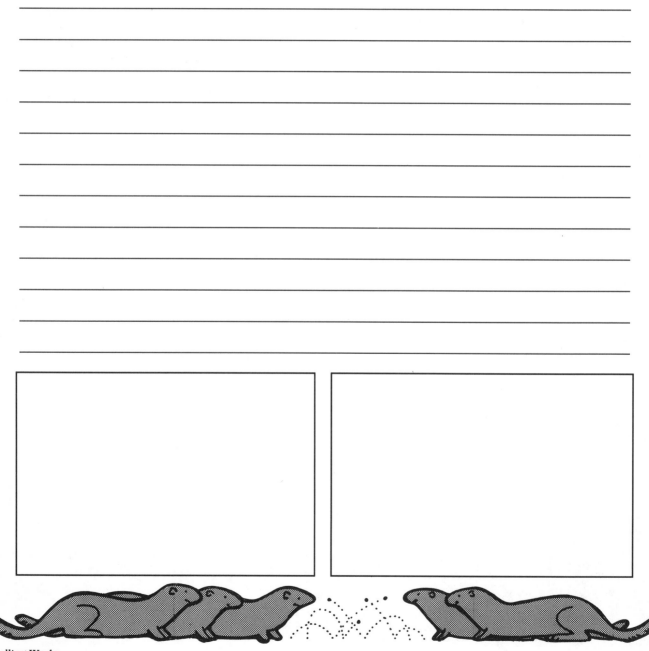

Word Discoveries

Select a word from your spelling list that contains a lot of letters. See how many smaller words you can make using only the letters in your chosen word.

Rules
1. The words you find must contain three or more letters.
2. Do not use proper nouns.
3. Plurals are allowed only if the letter **s** appears in your spelling word.
4. You may use letters only the number of times they appear in your spelling word.

Example: spelling word = **establishment**

    table is allowed but **tennis** is *not* allowed because there is only one **n** in the word establishment.

_____
spelling word

Use the back of your paper if you need more space. Try Word Discoveries for other words on your spelling list. Work together with a classmate to reach one hundred words for each spelling word you try.

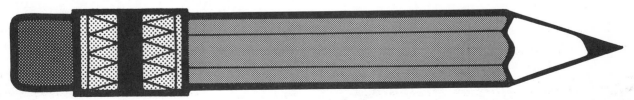

Spelling Works
©1993 – The Learning Works, Inc.

Word Stretchers

Using the words on your spelling list, see how many forms of each word you can write. Use the back of your paper if you need more space. Consult your dictionary if you need help.

Example: spelling word = **increase**

INCREASE
increasable
increased
increases
increasing
increasingly

Write a Rebus

A **rebus** is a puzzle made up of words or syllables that appear in the form of pictures. Pick eight of your spelling words. Create a rebus for each word. (The picture can represent a syllable in your word or the entire word.) Then, use the rebuses in a short story.

Examples:

budget

candidate

carpentry

childhood

diagnosis

graffiti

forceful

microscopic

superintendent

Create a Spelling Game

Create a board game using the words on your spelling list. Your game should include the following.

- an original name
- grade level for players (example: grades 4-6)
- object or purpose of your spelling game
- dice or spinner (directions on page 45)
- playing pieces for 2-4 players
- spelling words on index cards
- chance cards
- rules for play
- answer booklet (if necessary)
- playing board
- box for game contents

Paste your rules and directions inside the box cover. Your rules should answer the following questions:

a. What is the object of the spelling game?
b. Who goes first?
c. What do you do when you land on a square?
d. Who checks the answers in the answer booklet if one is used?
e. What happens if a spelling word is spelled correctly? Incorrectly?
f. When is the game over?

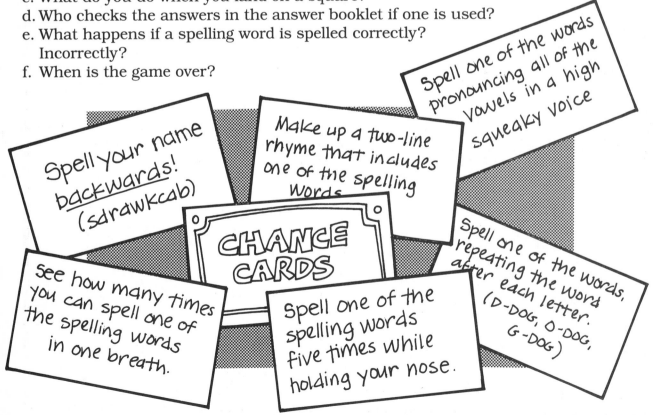

Create a Spelling Game
(continued)

How to Make a Spinner for Your Game

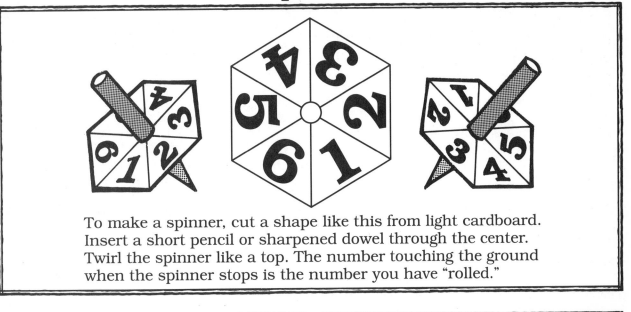

To make a spinner, cut a shape like this from light cardboard. Insert a short pencil or sharpened dowel through the center. Twirl the spinner like a top. The number touching the ground when the spinner stops is the number you have "rolled."

Sample Game Board

Sample Chance Cards

- Spell a word standing on one foot.
- Sing a spelling word to the tune of Happy Birthday.
- Spell the word and clap each time you come to a vowel.

Sample Rules

1. Spin the spinner to see how many spaces you can move.

2. If you land on a "C," take a chance card. If you land on an "S," take a card with a spelling word.

3. If you spell the word correctly, stay where you are until your next turn.

4. If you spell the word incorrectly, move back two squares.

Tricky Words to Spell

accede, *verb:* to agree
exceed, *verb:* to surpass

accept, *verb:* to receive
except, *verb:* to leave out

adapt, *verb:* to change or adjust
adept, *adv.:* expert, proficient, skillful
adopt, *verb:* to accept; to receive as one's own

affect, *verb:* to influence
effect, *verb:* to bring about
effect, *noun:* the result

aisle, *noun:* a passageway between sections of seats
isle, *noun:* a small island

all ready, *adj.:* completely prepared
already, *adv.:* before now, previously

allude, *verb:* to make brief or vague reference
elude, *verb:* to dodge or slip away from
illude, *verb:* to trick or deceive in the manner of a magician

allusion, *noun:* a reference
illusion, *noun:* something that deceives, misleads, or plays tricks upon

all ways, *adv.:* in every possible way
always, *adv.:* at all times; forever

annual, *adj.:* occurring yearly
biannual, *adj.:* occurring twice a year
biennial, *adj.:* occurring once every two years

ascent, *noun:* the act of climbing or going up
assent, *noun:* agreement or approval

assay, *verb:* to analyze or test
essay, *verb:* to attempt

avenge, *verb:* to punish in just payment for wrong done
revenge, *noun:* a personal attempt to get even

berth, *noun:* a resting place
birth, *noun:* the beginning of life

beside, *prep.:* at the side of; next to
besides, *prep.:* in addition to; moreover

capital, *noun:* a city that is the seat of government
capitol, *noun:* the building in which a legislative body deliberates

complement, *noun:* a completing part
compliment, *noun:* an expression of admiration

confidant, *noun:* a person in whom one confides
confident, *adj.:* certain

conscience, *noun:* sense of right
conscientious, *adj.:* governed by conscience; meticulous, careful
conscious, *adj.:* aware of an inward state and/or an outward fact

consul, *noun:* a government representative
council, *noun:* an assembly of persons convened for deliberation
counsel, *noun:* advice

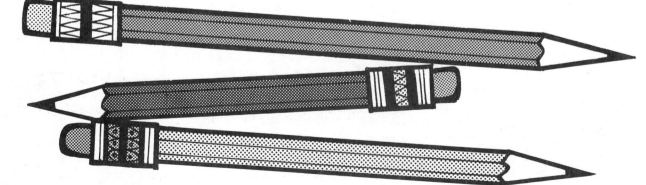

Tricky Words to Spell
(continued)

continual, *adj.:* recurring in steady and rapid succession

continuous, *adj.:* uninterrupted

decent, *adj.:* conforming to standards of propriety, good taste, or morality

descent, *noun:* the act of going from a higher to a lower level

dissent, *noun:* difference of opinion; disagreement

deduct, *verb:* to take away an amount or quantity from a total

subtract, *verb:* to take one number from another

deprecate, *verb:* to express disapproval or regret

depreciate, *verb:* to lessen in value

directions, *noun:* guidance or step-by-step instructions for reaching a goal, place, or destination

instructions, *noun:* an outline of procedures for the accomplishment of a task

discreet, *adj.:* wise, prudent, judicious

discrete, *adj.:* disconnected, separate

elicit, *verb:* to draw forth or bring out; to evoke

illicit, *adj.:* not permitted, unlawful

eliminate, *verb:* to get rid of

illuminate, *verb:* to supply with light

emigrate, *verb:* to leave one's own country for another

immigrate, *verb:* to come into a country of which one is not a native for permanent residence

former, *adj.:* the first of two

latter, *adj.:* the second of two; the end, last, or final

imply, *verb:* to express indirectly; to hint at or suggest

infer, *verb:* to draw a conclusion or conclusions based on facts or premises

incredible, *adj.:* unbelievable

incredulous, *adj.:* skeptical, disbelieving

ingenious, *adj.:* skillful in contriving; inventive

ingenuous, *adj.:* artless, naïve, innocent

lay, *verb:* to place

lie, *verb:* to recline

mania, *noun:* a craze

phobia, *noun:* a fear

persecute, *verb:* to oppress or harass

prosecute, *verb:* to initiate criminal action against

precede, *verb:* to be, come, or go ahead or in front of

proceed, *verb:* to continue after a pause; to go on in an orderly way

principal, *adj.:* most important

principal, *noun:* a chief or head man or woman

principle, *noun:* a rule or code of conduct

rout, *noun:* an overwhelming defeat

route, *noun:* a line or direction of travel

stationary, *adj.:* immovable

stationery, *noun:* letter paper and/or other materials for writing

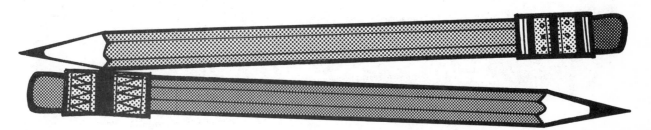

Spelling Works
©1993 – The Learning Works, Inc.

★SUPER★ SPELLER

_____
name

_____
date   **signature**

HEAR YE, HEAR YE

_____
is a sensational speller

_____
date   signature